Turn Conflict into Growth

Communication Strategies for Effective Mediation

Table of Contents

Chapter 1. Introduction

Special Report: **Turn Conflict into Growth: Communication Strategies for Effective Mediation**

We are thrilled to introduce "Turn Conflict into Growth: Communication Strategies for Effective Mediation," a groundbreaking Special Report that offers transformative insights into transforming conflict into opportunities for growth and development. This is not a highly technical dossier filled with jargon. It's a lively, impactful guide filled with practical strategies, relevant anecdotes, and real-world solutions to navigate through your personal or professional conflicts successfully. Each page is designed to be engaging and easy-to-understand, guiding you on a rich, enlightening journey towards becoming a skillful mediator. Let's put an end to persisting conflicts and invite harmony, growth, and progress! Secure your copy today and unlock the power of effective communication. This might be the best investment you make all year, sparking growth in areas you hadn't even considered. Learn, grow, navigate - it's all possible with "Turn Conflict into Growth."

Chapter 2. Understanding the Essence of Conflict

When it comes to understanding the essence of conflict, we ought to start with an appreciation of the dual nature of conflict as both an inevitable and potentially beneficial aspect of human connections. One of the foundational truths about conflict is that it isn't an inherently negative part of our lives. In fact, when handled effectively, conflict can be a powerful catalyst for growth, fostering deeper understanding, and underpinning stronger relationships.

2.1. Conflict: An Inescapable Reality

In the words of Carl Jung, "Everything that irritates us about others can lead us to an understanding of ourselves." The truth is, wherever there are human interaction, conflict is bound to occur. People have different needs, wants, values, and perspectives, often leading to disagreements and conflicts. Cultural, economic, and political contexts often color these individual differences, making conflict a complex, multi-layered matter.

2.2. The Role of Perception

One's perception of a situation plays a critical role in the escalation or the resolution of a conflict. Perception checks allow us to discern our misinterpretations and assumptions about other people's intentions. This critical tool can help us get to the true essence of the issue at hand. A shift in perspective often significantly impacts how we interpret and respond to conflicts.

2.3. Understanding Conflict Styles

Your conflict style, or the essential methodology you use to approach disagreements, can make a significant difference in the course of a conflict. There are five main conflict styles: competing, avoiding, accommodating, compromising, and collaborating. Each style has its pros and cons, and the effectiveness of each depends on the context of the conflict.

2.4. The Benefits of Constructive Conflict

Contrary to popular belief, conflict can be constructive, leading to numerous benefits when managed effectively. Constructive conflict can promote creativity, stimulate growth, and improve understanding and relationships. However, the crux lies in understanding the conditions under which conflict becomes a driver for positive outcomes - open-minded communication, a sense of fairness, and mutual respect.

2.5. The Dangers of Destructive Conflict

On the flip side, uncontrolled, or poorly managed conflict can spiral into destructive conflict. Here, the focus shifts from achieving a fair resolution to hurting the opponent and protecting oneself. This can lead to a breakdown in communication, broken relationships, and negative impacts on personal and organizational growth.

2.6. Conflict Resolution: A Life Skill

Understanding and approaching conflict in a mature and thoughtful manner is an invaluable life skill. It is profound and beneficial for personal development, effective teamwork, successful leadership, and even contributes to societal harmony.

With an understanding of the essence of conflict, we are better equipped to address disagreements when they arise and manage them in a way that facilitates growth and learning rather than division and discord. Such understanding, paired with robust communication strategies, forms the cornerstone of effective conflict resolution and, ultimately, personal and professional development.

2.7. Towards a Holistic Understanding

Understanding the essence of conflict is a holistic endeavor. It demands mindfulness of oneself, empathy towards others, and constant learning and adapting. As we explore more about communication strategies for mediation, the core knowledge of the relational, perceptual, and personal dimensions of conflict provides a foundational bedrock.

Knowledge of conflict in all its complexity is the first step in transforming such situations into opportunities for profound learning and growth. However, this knowledge must be translated into practice to navigate the rough waters of real-life conflict situations. The subsequent chapters will guide you in applying this understanding to actively turn conflict into growth.

Chapter 3. The Psychology of Mediation: Getting to the Heart of Conflict

In the realm of conflict resolution, understanding the psychological aspects underpinning disputes is critical. By grasping the complexity of human emotions, thought processes, and behaviors, we can develop more effective mediation strategies. Understanding these elements goes a long way in promoting empathy, fostering communication, and facilitating reconciliation in conflicting parties.

3.1. The Role of Emotions in Conflict

Conflict is inherently emotional. Parties involved often experience a range of strong feelings, including anger, fear, resentment, or even shame. These emotions not only fuel the conflict but also influence how each party perceives and responds to the situation. Accordingly, understanding emotional dynamics can aid a mediator to diffuse tension and encourage more constructive interaction.

In the mediation process, acknowledging emotions is essential. Let each party express their feelings, creating an environment where emotions are recognized as valid reactions rather than disregarded as irrational responses. This acceptance assists in establishing a respectful atmosphere, in turn reducing defensiveness and paving the way for open dialogue.

Conversely, when emotions are ignored, suppressed, or poorly handled, they can escalate the conflict significantly or engender ill feelings that linger long after the dispute is resolved. Hence, managing emotions is key to an effective resolution.

3.2. Cognitive Biases in Conflict Perception

Conflicts are not solely defined by the presenting issue but are also shaped by the perceptions and cognitions of the individuals involved. Cognitive biases, or systematic errors in thinking, significantly influence how parties perceive and approach conflicts.

Cognitive distortions such as 'confirmation bias' (favoring information that confirms pre-existing beliefs) and 'fundamental attribution error' (attributing other's actions to their character rather than external circumstances) can escalate disputes. Given such biases, parties often have skewed perceptions about the conflict, misjudge each other's intentions, and therefore resist conciliation.

It falls, then, upon the mediator to identify and challenge these biases. While doing so is not an easy task, techniques such as reframing or using neutral language can help the parties see the situation from a different perspective.

3.3. The Impact of Past Experiences

An individual's past experiences profoundly shape their psychological responses to conflict. If past conflicts have been resolved unsatisfactorily or were marked by intense emotionality, individuals might approach new disputes defensively or with dread. They might foresee conflict in negative terms or have a narrow perspective on resolution methods based on past experiences.

Understanding the parties' past experiences with conflict provides rich insight into their present reactions and attitudes. This understanding helps the mediator to tailor their approach to recognize and address these pre-existing fears and apprehensions, making sure they don't hinder the mediation process.

3.4. Communication Styles in Conflict

Communication style is another psychological aspect of utmost importance in conflict situations. Verbal and nonverbal cues can either soothe or exacerbate tensions. Positive communication behaviors, such as active listening, expressing empathy, and maintaining open body language, dramatically enhance the chances of successful mediation. On the contrary, negative behaviors like interrupting, blaming, or showing contempt can push parties further apart.

A mediator must, therefore, foster a communicative environment that encourages understanding, empathy, and cooperation. Modelling positive communication behaviors and firmly discouraging negative ones can go a long way in achieving a successful resolution.

3.5. The Psychology of Forgiveness and Reconciliation

Finally, understanding the psychology of forgiveness and reconciliation is important. Encouraging these elements often sets the foundation for long-term conflict resolution. Emotional forgiveness, in which parties replace negative emotions with understanding and compassion, and decisional forgiveness, where they make a conscious choice to avoid revenge and ill-will, are both crucial for reconciliation. A skilled mediator can facilitate these processes by validating feelings of hurt and guiding parties towards empathizing with each other's perspectives.

In conclusion, successful mediation is profoundly rooted in understanding the psychology of conflict. By sensitively addressing emotions, cognitive biases, past experiences, communication styles, and fostering forgiveness and reconciliation, it's possible for a mediator to turn a situation of conflict into one of growth and progress.

Chapter 4. Architects of Balance: The Role of Mediators

It's an age-old truth that mediators play an integral role in managing conflict situations, where both parties are often emotionally involved or invested. However, the art and science behind this critical profession reach far beyond merely acting as a neutral third party. Indeed, the mediator's actual role is akin to an architect of balance, carefully navigating the temperaments, differences, and complexities inherent in the very fabric of human discourse to foster a harmonious resolution.

4.1. The Nature of Mediation

At its core, mediation is a process of facilitated negotiation. It increases communication, eradicates misunderstandings, and cultivates a meaningful dialogue between parties stuck in conflict. Mediators need not be arbiters of truth who determine right from wrong but rather facilitators who create a conducive environment for productive discussions.

Mediators acknowledge the subjective perceptions of all individuals involved in the dispute and strive to unearth the underlying emotions, interests, and values that are often masked by rigid stances and positions. They strive to dial down the intensity of confrontations and morph hostility into dialogue.

4.2. Mediators as Conversation Catalysts

One of the critical functions of mediators lies in enabling conversation. Not just any conversation, but one that respects each party's feelings and perspectives, promoting understanding. They pave the way for parties to express their concerns freely, fostering an atmosphere of empathy and acceptance rather than a battleground for proving who is right or wrong. In essence, they facilitate a shift from positioning ("I am right") to interest-seeking conversations ("How do we resolve this").

Mediators manage the process by using an array of effective communication techniques. Through active listening, they enable each party to feel heard, thereby simultaneously garnering critical insights into the heart of the matter. Moreover, they make use of powerful questioning, enabling participants to step back from entrenched positions and consider alternatives.

4.3. The Power of Neutral Territory

Another crucial aspect of a mediator's role lies in providing neutral territory for the parties involved in a feud. The mere act of bringing opposing parties together in a neutral place, free from the daily hierarchies or stressful factors, can dramatically shift the dynamics of conflict.

Also, mediators are often seen as neutral figures without any vested interest in the matter at hand. They do not take sides or make decisions but, instead, aid the parties in finding a resolution they both can accept. This neutrality emblematically converts the mediator's space into a 'safe-zone' for candid interactions, devoid of judgment or repercussions.

4.4. Stringing the Story

A mediator also performs the art of "narrative mediation," a process of the storyline, unraveling the threads of conflict. Unlike traditional forms of dispute resolution, where rules and facts dictate the method, narrative mediation digs deeper. It delves into the stories that individuals involved in the conflict have about themselves and the other parties.

By inviting different perspectives through storytelling, an environment conducive to empathy and understanding can be set. As each party reveals their version of the story, mediators can help them recognize the influence of their narrations on their relationship and the conflict. They guide the parties to rewrite the story by highlighting the forgotten or hidden areas of agreement, cooperation, and positive interaction which conflict shadowed.

4.5. Emotional Intelligence: The Silent Fuel of Mediation

The underlying force that powers successful mediations is the mediator's emotional intelligence. A skilled mediator leverages emotional intelligence to create an environment of trust where people can share their deepest concerns without fear of judgment or penalty.

This quality allows mediators to accurately perceive, understand, and regulate emotions in the mediation environment, thereby controlling conflict escalation. They know when to listen quietly, when to empathize, and when to press for more clarity, demonstrating both patience and resilience.

Every conversation in mediation is an opportunity for growth. This report provides a treasury of actionable strategies and techniques that can aid you in becoming an effective architect of balance. By using these methods, you can help parties to unravel their conflicts, frame their stories, and navigate their way towards a mutually acceptable resolution.

Turn the conflict into growth. Empower yourself with these tools, change lives, and orchestrate harmony in contrast to being shackled by discord and misunderstanding.

Chapter 5. A Toolkit for Effective Communication: Getting Your Message Across

Effective communication is a critical tool in any mediation process. It empowers individuals to express their perspectives, needs, and concerns clearly, enabling better understanding and mutual respect. The strategies, techniques, and insights below will equip you with the knowledge and skills to communicate your message effectively.

5.1. Understanding the Communication Process

Communication occurs more precisely when the message sent aligns with the message received. Three basic components shape this process: the sender, the receiver, and the message itself. Understanding these components is crucial in formulating an impactful conveyance of your perspective.

1. **Sender**: The sender is the origin of the communication. The ability of the sender to articulate their views clearly and accurately will significantly affect whether the message is understood correctly.

2. **Receiver**: The receiver is the individual who deciphers the message. They interpret this message through their filters, including emotion, bias, and personal experience.

3. **Message**: The message refers to the information or sentiment expressed by the sender.

Precise communication emerges from the seamless function of these elements, facilitating clear understanding between parties.

5.2. Effective Ways of Conveying Your Message

Packaging your message is vital to its proper reception. Various strategies, including simplifying complex ideas and structuring arguments logically, contribute to effectively conveying your message.

1. **Clarity**: Ensure your message is free of ambiguity and is direct, succinct, and clear.

2. **Know Your Audience**: Tailor your message to the audience's level of understanding. Speak in a language familiar to them, utilizing examples that resonate with their experiences.

3. **Be Assertive, Not Aggressive**: An assertive communication style respects the opinions of others while firmly stating your own.

4. **Logical Structure**: Arrange your ideas logically to make them easy to follow.

5. **Active Listening**: Active listening establishes a two-way communication pattern, encouraging the receiver's engagement and facilitating mutual understanding.

5.3. The Role of Non-Verbal Communication

Non-verbal communication includes all the information conveyed aside from the words themselves. This form of communication can bolster the effectiveness of your message when used appropriately.

1. **Posture**: Maintaining an open and relaxed posture conveys receptivity and attentiveness.

2. **Facial Expression**: Facial expressions can communicate emotional content, reinforcing or contradicting the spoken

message.

3. **Gestures**: Gestures such as nodding, pointing, or crossing arms speak volumes about attitudes and feelings.

4. **Eye Contact**: Establishing and maintaining good eye contact signifies interest and sincerity.

5. **Tone of Voice**: The way words are spoken greatly impacts the message's meaning. Paying attention to tone catalyzes clearer conversations.

5.4. Communicating Effectively in Difficult Situations

Communicating in high-stress situations requires a unique skill set. These strategies enable communication effectiveness and minimize misunderstandings during conflicts.

1. **Stay Calm**: Losing control may convey disrespect and escalate the situation. Breathe, manage your reactions, and maintain composure.

2. **Avoid Defensiveness**: Defensive responses could perpetuate the conflict. Aim to understand the other party's viewpoint without resorting to defence mechanisms.

3. **Time Out**: If discussions become heated, suggest taking a break to calm down before resuming.

4. **Solution-Focused Dialogue**: Shift the conversation from past mistakes to future solutions.

5.5. Implementing Communication Technology

Modern technology facilitates seamless, real-time communication. Be sure to adapt to these technologies effectively and ethically.

1. **Selecting the Right Tool**: Choose communication tools conducive to the conversational needs. Video calls might be more suitable for complex discussions, while instant messaging can cater to quick, simple exchanges.

2. **Netiquette**: Good online etiquette involves respectful communication, refraining from using ALL CAPS (which communicates yelling), and promptly responding to messages.

3. **Security and Privacy**: Ensure all communication platforms use strong encryption to protect sensitive information shared.

In summation, mastering the art of communication can significantly enhance your ability to navigate conflicts. From verbal acuity, non-verbal cues, to the optimal use of technology, each plays a part in guiding the outcome of your conversations. By applying these strategies, you can ensure that your message not only reaches its destination but lands with the desired impact.

Chapter 6. Navigating Emotional Barriers: Empathy in Mediation

In the curious arena of conflict resolution, one of the most profound areas to explore is the role of emotional barriers in the process of mediation. Emotions can be both a catalyst and a wall, preventing a peaceful resolution, or driving a positive, shared future. Their impact is vast and tactile. The key to navigating these emotional obstacles lies in empathy, the soft skill widely proclaimed as the core of effective mediation.

6.1. The Role of Empathy in Mediation

One of the foundational principles of mediation is understanding the emotions of the involved parties. Emotion drives behavior, and behavior drives conflict or resolution. Empathy, in this context, plays an instrumental role as it enables mediators to connect with those emotions, explore them without judgment, and guide parties towards a mutually beneficial resolution.

Empathy helps establish a trustful environment where parties can feel safe expressing their views without fear of ridicule or dismissal. By portraying an empathetic stance, mediators project a sense of commitment to their roles and show parties they genuinely care about the outcomes of the conflict resolution.

6.2. Understanding Emotional Barriers

An emotional barrier is anything that prevents us from communicating our true thoughts and feelings. These are internal obstructions that deter us from expressing our innermost feelings for fear of embarrassment, guilt, or offending others. Emotional barriers, such as anger, resentment, or fear, are powerful deterrents that can thwart an individual's contribution to the conflict resolution.

To circumvent these barriers, mediators need to build a comforting bridge of empathic connections. The first step is to acknowledge these emotions by allowing parties to openly express their feelings about the conflict. Creating space for emotional expression gives parties a sense of being understood and acknowledged, helping them to lower their defenses and engage more openly in the discussion.

6.3. Methods to Cultivate Empathy

Becoming empathetic is not an overnight process. It involves the cultivation of many skills, including active listening, nonverbal communication, and emotional intelligence. Each of these aspects contributes to a richer empathetic understanding.

1. **Active Listening**: This involves truly understanding the speaker's message. It includes paraphrasing their words, reflecting them back to show understanding, and confirming interpretations.

2. **Nonverbal Communication**: This relates to understanding the sentiments expressed through body language, facial expressions, or other non-spoken forms of communication. A gentle nod, maintaining eye contact, or an attentive posture can convey understanding and care.

3. **Emotional Intelligence**: This refers to understanding and

managing one's own emotions and accurately picking up the emotions of others. Greater emotional intelligence supports empathy by fostering an ability to connect with the emotional state of others.

Invest time and effort in learning these skills. The growth experienced will not only aid in being a better mediator but will also contribute to personal development.

6.4. Applying Empathy in Mediation Practices

After understanding the importance of empathy and the methods to cultivate it, let's look at how it can be applied in mediation practices. Empathy becomes a tool for mediators to work through the emotional barriers present and pave a path towards conflict resolution.

1. **Encourage Emotional Expression**: Give room for parties to express their emotions freely. Refrain from judgment or criticism, facilitating a safe and open environment.

2. **Remain Neutral**: While encouraging emotional expression, maintain neutrality. You are there to understand, not to take sides.

3. **Mirror Understanding**: Show understanding and confirmation of feelings. This action enables parties to see that their emotions are being acknowledged.

4. **Guide Emotional Discharges**: Help guide emotional discharges in a productive manner, away from resentment or anger, and towards understanding and resolution.

Your empathy is not just a tool; it's also a symbol of authenticity and genuineness in the mediation process. It highlights your interest in and commitment to the parties' emotional conditions and their strife for resolution.

6.5. Transforming Emotional Barriers into Stepping Stones

Lastly, it's essential to not view emotional barriers as unavoidable roadblocks but rather as stepping stones towards growth both for the parties and the mediator. If navigated correctly through empathy, these emotions can be instrumental in fostering deeper understanding, establishing stronger connections, and leading towards a satisfactory resolution that goes beyond the superficial scope of conflict.

Remember, every emotion is a message deftly packed with insights that offer a glimpse into the mind of the person experiencing it. By understanding, acknowledging, and empathizing with these emotional barriers, mediators not just broker peace, but they also facilitate growth, feeding into the development of relationships and building stronger individuals in the process.

In conclusion, empathy is undeniably a potent tool in the mediator's arsenal to navigate emotional barriers. With practice and careful application, mediators can truly turn these perceived obstacles into an opportunity for growth and resolution - transforming not just conflicts, but also impacting lives in a profound, positive manner.

Chapter 7. Resolving Conflict via Active Listening

Active listening is a foundational communication technique that involves fully focusing, understanding, responding, and subsequently, remembering what is being said. It is significantly different from passive hearing and requires an explicit and mindful effort from the listener. Let's delve deep into the world of active listening and understand how it can be an effective tool to resolve conflicts.

7.1. The Art and Science of Active Listening

Active listening is both an art and a science. As an art, it requires creativity, insight, and a sense of understanding to be able to 'tune in' fully to the speaker. The listener has to put aside their own thoughts, preconceptions, and judgments to be truly present for the speaker. This includes avoiding thinking about responses, mentally agreeing or disagreeing, or making judgments about the speaker's intelligence or capabilities.

On the scientific side, active listening is about understanding human communication, its barriers and filters. It involves learning the steps of the process, practicing them, and using feedback to improve.

There are four primary steps to active listening:

1. Understand the message
2. Offer feedback
3. Defer judgment
4. Respond appropriately

7.2. Understanding the Message

Understanding involves listening for the essence of what the speaker is saying, not just the words. This takes focus, as it's easy, especially in a tense situation, to become caught up in your interpretation and reaction to the message. Understanding means asking clarifying questions, paraphrasing what the speaker is saying, and summarizing their points for them to verify accuracy.

7.3. Offering Feedback

Feedback refers to a response that confirms what you heard and how you understood it. Feedback does not mean agreement or disagreement. It is just a way to confirm understanding.

Here are some techniques to offer effective feedback:

- Reflecting: Reflect the speaker's emotions. "You sound frustrated with this situation."

- Paraphrasing: Restate the speaker's key points in your own words. "So, you're saying that you're not getting the support you need from your team."

- Questioning: Ask questions to clarify certain points. "What do you mean when you say 'overbearing'? Could you give me some examples?"

Try to keep your questions open-ended, to encourage the speaker to explore their feelings and thoughts.

7.4. Deferring Judgment

A significant part of active listening is a non-judgmental disposition. Deferring judgement not only upholds the speaker's dignity but also encourages them to share openly. This catalyzes conflict resolution.

Here are few steps on how to defer judgement:

1. Distance yourself from your personal opinions.

2. Try not to take everything personally. Remind yourself that it's not about you.

3. Be open to new ideas and perspectives.

4. Focus on their words, tone, and body language, not how you feel about them.

Developing a non-judgmental mindset is a journey that requires practice and patience but leads to more effective communication and conflict resolution.

7.5. Responding Appropriately

The last step is to respond in a way that communicates understanding and respect. It involves validating the speaker's feelings and emotions, showing empathy, and indicating understanding. If you have any dissent or different point of view, communicate it with respect, focusing on the issue and not on the person.

7.6. Overcoming Listening Barriers

Active listening is not an easy skill and there are numerous barriers that can interfere with its successful execution. The good news is that all of them can be overcome with awareness and practice. Some common barriers include distractions, biases, and defensive listening.

Distractions could be internal or external — from your thoughts to the environment around you. In this case, it helps to be mindful, present, and in the moment.

Biases, on the other hand, can be tricky. Each one of us has biases, and they may influence our listening. It helps to be aware of them so we can ensure they do not act as barriers.

Lastly, defensive listening, where you focus on defending your position rather than understanding the other's perspective, can be a major roadblock. Try to stay open and receptive, focusing on mutual respect and understanding.

7.7. Listening, Understanding, and Mediating

Active listening makes the speaker feel valued and understood, promoting a positive emotional climate conducive to conflict resolution. It also makes it possible for mediators to understand deeply, dissect the conflict and propose solutions that are acceptable to both parties.

Understand that conflicts cannot be resolved in haste. They require patience, understanding, and the potential for uncomfortable conversations. Active listening in these instances acts as a soothing balm, keeping tempers in check, and paving the way for resolution.

In conclusion, extend your ear, your mind, and your heart to the speaker. Truly listen. Let your silence speak louder than words – it says "I respect you, I am interested in what you are saying and I am in this discussion for a meaningful dialogue." Combine this with the ability to mediate discussions and watch how conflicts find their solutions in the most harmonious ways.

Chapter 8. Transforming Discord into Dialogue: The Power of Words

There's a powerful, transformational potential resting within our language. The words we use, the phrases we pick, the tone we adopt - all these factors can turn a potentially destructive discord into a fruitful dialogue. With the right set of strategies, anyone can harness this power to foster understanding, collaboration, and mutual growth.

Let's delve into this fascinating exploration.

8.1. Understanding the Power of Words

Words have a profound impact on how we interpret the world and relate with others. According to the renowned linguist Noam Chomsky, language is not just a medium of communication, but also a framework for our thoughts. Hence, when we use a certain type of language during a conflict, it not just reflects our emotions but also shapes our reaction.

Negative and hostile words can be inflammatory and push the dispute further, while positive and constructive words can turn the tide, opening channels for dialogue and resolution. However, the challenge lies in channeling this power during a contentious situation, which requires conscious effort, practice, and strategical thinking.

8.2. Active Listening: A Catalyst for Constructive Communication

One of the key elements for transforming discord into dialogue is active listening, which means actively understanding the other person's perspective and acknowledging their needs and feelings.

Active listening is a manifestation of empathy and respect towards the speaker. It can help diffusing the tension, allowing a more constructive and focused conversation on the problem at hand, rather than the emotions it's generating.

There are few practices that can help you embrace active listening: . Giving undivided attention to the speaker. . Using verbal nods such as 'uh-huh,' 'right,' 'I see' to show that you're actively listening. . Paraphrasing and reflecting back the speaker's words to ensure you have understood properly. . Asking open-ended questions to clarify. . Avoiding interruptions before the speaker completes his/her thought.

Remember, active listening doesn't mean that you are agreeing with the other person, rather it's about understanding their perspective thoroughly before proposing your viewpoint.

8.3. Language of Empathy: Encouraging a Mutual Exchange

Empathetic language is a pathway to bring down the walls individuals might have built during the conflict. Expressions of empathy such as 'I understand where you're coming from,' 'I see why this is important to you,' and 'I appreciate your viewpoint on this' can give the other person a sense of validation and reassurance. With these minor modifications in our language, we foster an environment that encourages mutual exchange of ideas and respectfully disagrees without personally attacking.

8.4. The Role of Non-Verbal Communication

Non-verbal communication – body language, posture, eye contact, tone of voice– plays a significant role in mediating conversations. Especially during conflicts, when emotions are running high, your body language and tone can portray respect, openness and patience. Maintaining neutral body language, an even tone of voice, ensuring eye contact, can contribute significantly to de-escalating the situation.

8.5. The Art of Framing

Framing is a powerful technique that can divert the course of a conflict. By shifting the focus from blaming each other to focusing on the problem and how to resolve it, you can create a collaborative environment. Use mutual language such as 'we', 'us', 'our' that promotes camaraderie and focuses on the problem rather than individuals.

8.6. Mirroring: Reflecting for Respect and Understanding

Mirroring takes active listening a step further. It's the act of reflecting the speaker's tone, pace, body language, and choice of words. It is subtle, and not simply mimicry. The key here is to naturally reflect in a way that makes the speaker feel comfortable and acknowledged. This opens up a safe space for both parties to express themselves freely and respectfully.

8.7. The Power of Patience

Patience is a virtue, particularly in the process of transforming discord into dialogue. Often during a conflict, we're rushed to share our points, justify our stance, and rush towards a resolution. This hurried approach can overlook the intricacies of the problem and miss the opportunity for true dialogue and deeper understanding. Taking your time to listen, understand, and respond can foster patience and encourage a calm, meaningful dialogue.

By intertwining these strategies into our communication, we essentially enable ourselves and others to approach conflicts not as threats to our ego or self-expression, but as opportunities to grow, learn, and foster mutual respect. Transforming discord into a fruitful exchange of ideas and emotions is no small task, but it's an essential step for growth in any personal or professional relationship.

As you engage with your next conflict, remember, the power of transformation is lodged in your words and the ways you use them. You can either fan the flames or douse them with understanding and empathy. The choice, as always, is entirely yours.

Chapter 9. Cultivating a Resolution-Focused Mindset: Turning Obstacles into Opportunities

Conflicts tend to be viewed as undesired situations that we should avoid or quickly resolve. Yet, if approached with the right mindset and effective communication tools, these so-called obstacles can be transformed into opportunities for growth — both personal and professional.

9.1. The Resolution-Focused Mindset

Recognizing the potential for growth within conflict begins with shifting your mindset from problem-focused to resolution-focused. A problem-focused perspective emphasizes the negatives of a situation, often leading to defensive reactions and escalating tension. In contrast, a resolution-focused view reframes the situation as a challenge, stimulating constructive dialogue, mutual understanding, and finding potential improvements.

Imagine a situation where you and your colleague have divergent views about project execution methods. While your colleague prefers a traditional, structured approach, you are a devotee of agile methodologies. A problem-focused mindset perceives this difference as an obstacle, potentially leading to futile debates and increased pressures. On the other hand, a resolution-focused approach frames the disagreement as an opportunity to borrow from both processes, to develop a hybrid model that yields better results.

9.2. Developing Your Resolution-Focused Perspective

Building a resolution-focused mindset doesn't happen overnight; it's a muscle that requires continuous conscious development. Here are a few exercises to help:

Key Exercise 1: When faced with a conflict, pause, and analyze the situation. Are you reacting or responding? Reactions are often instant, driven by the subconscious mind and charged with emotion. Responses, however, are slower, calculated, and more logical — a cornerstone for resolution-focused thinking.

Key Exercise 2: Regularly engage in self-reflection. This practice enables you to understand your emotional triggers, biases, and patterns in conflict resolution. Journaling or meditating on past conflicts from a resolution-focused perspective can provide sharp insights.

Key Exercise 3: Practice active listening and empathy. By understanding the other party's point of view, you cultivate patience, tolerance, and creativity — attributes essential to resolution-focused thinking.

Key Exercise 4: Continually engage in cognitive restructuring. The idea here is to replace negative thought patterns with more positive and constructive ones. This reshaping eventually aligns your instinctive responses with a resolution-focused perspective.

9.3. Turning Obstacles into Opportunities

With a well-cultivated resolution-focused perspective, we can now delve into turning conflicts into opportunities for growth:

A Shift in Perspective: Treat every conflict as a learning opportunity, a chance to broaden your understanding, engage creatively with problems, and adapt to new perspectives.

Creating a New Narrative: The stories we tell ourselves play a crucial role in how we perceive and handle conflicts. Therefore, creating a new narrative is about changing our dialogue from antagonism to mutuality, from problems to solutions.

Finding the Silver Lining: Every conflict, however bitter, always has a silver lining. Find this hidden opportunity, as it often leads to profound personal growth and professional development.

Embracing Discomfort: Growth rarely happens within the comfort zone. Embrace the discomfort that conflict brings; it's part of the process leading to growth.

9.4. Conclusion

In cultivating a resolution-focused mindset, it's essential to remember small everyday practices can cause significant shifts in one's approach towards conflicts. By persistently developing this mindset and viewing conflicts as opportunities, we can encourage growth, harmony, and progress in our personal and professional lives. Remember, the difference between an obstacle and an opportunity lies in the perspective.

Chapter 10. Case Studies: Successful Mediation and Conflict Transformation

The real beauty of mediation lies in its capacity to transform the seemingly stalemated conflicts into an opportunity for growth. A closer look at successful instances of mediation and conflict resolution could provide invaluable insights into the process and its outcomes. Here are some of these case studies!

10.1. The Skilled Mediator: Transforming the Boardroom Conflict

Jane was a highly skilled mediator, renowned for her ability to transform conflicts. She was chosen to mediate a dispute within a large corporation, where the board of directors were in a deadlock over a strategic business decision. She began her mediation by facilitating dialogue. She guided each director to express their thoughts and concerns openly, creating an atmosphere of understanding and mutual respect.

Despite evident differences in viewpoints, Jane successfully helped them find common ground. She used the "value finding process," where the directors were encouraged to identify shared values and preferences. The board of directors was able to identify a unified goal - maximizing the organization's success. With this understanding, they were able to brainstorm solutions together, leading to a resolution that best fitted their shared values.

In the end, an initially heated conflict was transformed into an opportunity for the board to understand their common values better, resulting in a more cohesive, unified decision-making body.

10.2. The Teacher's Intervention: Mediating Student Conflicts

Sarah, an experienced high school teacher, was often tasked with mediating conflicts among her students. In one instance, a conflict arose between two students, Tom and Jerry, regarding a group project. A series of misunderstandings had led them to cease communication, adversely affecting their project's progress.

Sarah sought to mediate by initially conversing with Tom and Jerry separately. She ensured that they were given a safe platform to share their feelings and thoughts. These initial individual sessions helped to unearth the core issues that had led to misunderstanding. Sarah then brought them together for a joint session. She facilitated a respectful discussion where they could openly express their feelings and concerns. Sarah made sure that everyone's perspectives were heard and respected, and that they understood each other's viewpoints.

Through this process, Tom and Jerry were able to see beyond their conflict and recognized their common aim - producing quality output for their group project. They managed to establish a more effective, collaborative relationship and successfully completed the project.

10.3. Global Mediation: Resolving International Disputes

Mediation goes beyond boardrooms and classrooms. It has been used as an effective diplomatic tool to resolve international disputes. A classic case is the Camp David Accords. Presidents Anwar Sadat of Egypt and Menachem Begin of Israel were in conflict over the land taken by Israel during the 1967 war. American President Jimmy Carter acted as the mediator.

Carter knew the key to successful mediation lay in understanding the needs of both parties. He mediated over a span of thirteen days, helping each nation clarify their needs and understand each other's perspectives. This discussion paved the way for the leaders to find mutually beneficial solutions. The Camp David Accords ended with a peace treaty signed by Begin and Sadat, marking the end of thirty years of hostilities between Egypt and Israel.

In these scenarios, mediation served as a mechanism to transform conflicts into opportunities for enhanced understanding and more robust cooperation. The essence of mediation is finding a common ground, promoting empathy, and fostering open communication.

At times, conflicts are inevitable. However, viewing conflict as a chance for improvement rather than a hurdle can bring about significant growth. As we navigate through our lives, whether we're a senior executive in a boardroom, students in a classroom, or nations on the global stage, the ability to effectively manage and mediate conflicts will invariably prove to be a key asset.

Chapter 11. Embracing Growth: Conflict as a Catalyst for Change

The understanding of conflict as an obstacle is deeply ingrained in our minds. However, this perspective can be limiting and unproductive. Viewing conflict as a catalyst for change disentangles us from the belief that conflict is only negative. It encourages growth, improvement, and innovation. One just needs to understand that conflict, when handled correctly, can become a driver of personal and professional growth.

11.1. Embracing a Growth Mindset

The concept of a growth mindset, introduced by psychologist Carol Dweck, is a critical paradigm in turning conflict into a catalyst for change. It posits that individuals who believe their talents can be developed (through hard work, good strategies, and input from others) have a growth mindset. They tend to achieve more than those with a more fixed mindset who believe their talents are innate gifts.

In the face of conflict, a growth mindset enables us to see it not as an insurmountable problem but as an opportunity for growth, learning, and development. This perspective shift is key to enabling growth amidst tensions and disagreements. It demands perseverance, resilience, and a continuous learning attitude, all of which can transform us into a better version of ourselves.

11.2. Conflict as a Catalyst: The Science Behind It

Underlying this understanding of conflict as a catalyst for change is the concept of constructive conflict. Constructive conflict refers to conflict in which the benefits exceed the costs; it generates productive, mutually beneficial, shared decisions.

This constructive conflict can stimulate creativity and innovation, promote understanding and cooperation among team members, and aid in the identification and correction of mistakes. It encourages individuals and teams to view problems from different perspectives and come up with novel solutions.

Conflict stimulates stress and pressure that, within manageable levels, can boost productivity and performance. This principle is based on the Yerkes-Dodson law, which suggests that performance increases with physiological or mental arousal (stress) but only up to a point. When the stress becomes too high, performance decreases.

11.3. Developing Effective Conflict Resolution Skills

Turning conflict into a catalyst for personal and professional growth involves developing effective conflict resolution skills at an individual and team level. These skills include active listening, clear and calm communication, emotional intelligence and empathy, objectivity, patience and perseverance, and problem-solving.

Active listening involves fully focusing, understanding, and responding to the speaker. It's about understanding the underlying emotions and messages. Clear and calm communication involves being concise, precise, and articulate in conveying your thoughts, emotions, and propositions.

Emotional intelligence and empathy entail recognizing and understanding your emotions and those of others, and using this awareness to manage behavior and relationships. It is about putting oneself in others' shoes to understand their perspectives better.

Objectivity involves taking a balanced view of the situation, devoid of personal biases and prejudices. Patience and perseverance mean being steadfast in the face of adversity and uncertainty, committing to the resolution process even if it gets prolonged.

Finally, problem-solving involves recognizing and defining the conflict, generating and evaluating potential solutions, deciding on the most effective solution, implementing it, and evaluating the effectiveness of the solution.

11.4. Navigating Professional Conflict

When it comes to the work environment, conflicts are inevitable. Different viewpoints, perspectives, priorities, and ways of functioning can all lead to disagreements. However, these should not be seen as detrimental. On the contrary, they should be seen as opportunities for growth and improvement.

Disagreements can prompt us to reevaluate our existing methods, make necessary changes, and explore new possibilities. They can help us to innovate, improve our services or products, foster teamwork, and improve the overall performance of the organization.

To harness the positive potential of conflict in a professional setting, it is essential to foster an open and safe environment where everyone feels comfortable expressing their ideas and concerns. This requires effective leadership that encourages open communication, mutual respect, and a growth mindset across the organization.

Conflict, when utilized positively, can be transformative. It is a moment to pause, reflect, learn, grow, and innovate. It is an opportunity to better oneself, improve relations with others, and make strides in personal and professional growth. Literature has often equated conflict with the necessary friction that is required to produce the pearl. With the right outreach, that pearl could well be a newfound reservoir of creativity, collaboration, and commitment to growth.

www.ingramcontent.com/pod-product-compliance
Lightning Source LLC
Chambersburg PA
CBHW072220290526
45794CB00007B/2825